Eating Disorders

A Hot Issue

David Goodnough

HOT
ISSUES

Enslow Publishers, Inc.

40 Industrial Road	PO Box 38
Box 398	Aldershot
Berkeley Heights, NJ 07922	Hants GU12 6BP
USA	UK

http://www.enslow.com

Library of Congress Cataloging-in-Publication Data

Goodnough, David.
    Eating disorders : a hot issue / David Goodnough.
       p. cm. — (Hot issues)
    Includes bibliographical references and index.
    Summary: Discusses various eating disorders, with an emphasis on anorexia nervosa and bulimia nervosa, and tells the stories of people who have suffered from them.
    ISBN 0-7660-1336-7
    1. Eating disorders—Juvenile literature. 2. Bulimia—Juvenile literature. 3. Anorexia nervosa—Juvenile literature. [1. Anorexia nervosa. 2. Bulimia. 3. Eating disorders.]
    I. Title. II. Series.
    RC552. E18G66   1999
    616.85'26—dc21   98-34057
                                     CIP
                                     AC

Printed in the United States of America

10 9 8 7 6 5 4 3 2 1

To Our Readers:
All Internet Addresses in this book were active and appropriate when we went to press. Any comments or suggestions can be sent by e-mail to Comments@enslow.com or to the address on the back cover.

Illustration Credits:
AP/Wide World Photos/C. J. Gunther, p. 45; AP/Wide World Photos/Eric Risberg, p. 8; AP/Wide World Photos/John Parkin, p. 53; AP/Wide World Photos/Roberto Borea, p. 18; AP/Wide World Photos/Shawn Baldwin, WPA Rota, p. 30; AP/Wide World Photos, pp. 17, 47; © Corel Corporation, pp. 1, 4, 12, 16, 28, 38.

Cover Illustration: Enslow Publishers, Inc.

Contents

*E*ating disorders can develop when young women diet to look like the extremely thin models they see in magazines and on television.

Chapter 1

A Baffling Illness

Jennifer was sixteen years old. She was a lively, popular girl who maintained good grades in her high school classes and participated in extracurricular activities. She was not too interested in boys and was close to a group of her girl classmates. She played the clarinet and was a member of the high school marching band. She especially enjoyed taking part in the halftime entertainment during her school's football games.

When the band finally got new uniforms after a long fund-raising campaign, some of the girls in the band thought that their uniforms didn't fit well and decided to go on diets. They thought that it would improve the overall appearance of the band if all the girls looked about the same size and that their uniforms fit perfectly.

Jennifer's uniform fit her, but she decided to go along with the diet because everyone else was doing it, and she wanted to join in. It seemed to be a lot of fun comparing what and how much they had eaten and how much weight each girl had lost from day to day or from week to week. Jennifer began to lose weight. Her parents were very health conscious, and they approved of Jennifer's new interest in food. Jennifer began to consult cookbooks and books on dieting and physical fitness. At first, her parents were delighted, but then they began to be worried about Jennifer's noticeable weight loss.

Jennifer's new thinness emphasized the smallness of her breasts. Her buttocks, which had never appeared large before, now stood out in contrast to the rest of her body. Her classmates began to tease her, making comments on her small "boobs" and big "butt." Jennifer became self-conscious and withdrew into her schoolwork and her new interest in food preparation. She was fascinated with food but not with eating it. She knew she was growing very thin, but she continued to diet. She felt that if she started eating foods that she had been avoiding, she would get fat in those parts of her body that she was teased about.

Jennifer continued to lose weight. Her hair became dull and brittle, and her skin became dry and scaly. She became constipated and felt weak and listless. Her period stopped. This alarmed her mother, and she insisted that Jennifer see a doctor.

Jennifer was diagnosed as having anorexia nervosa, an eating disorder in which people starve themselves or eat very little in order to lose weight. It occurs mainly in preteen or adolescent girls and young women.

It can be a passing phase or a severe, life-threatening illness. Jennifer was lucky, because her disorder was recognized early. Her doctor suggested professional help. Jennifer was hospitalized for "refeeding," which involved eating under close watch. It was not successful. She did respond, however, to counseling and at-home treatment by a therapist. She began slowly to regain weight and to return to her interests in school and music.

Jennifer shows signs of having recovered and has taken an interest in social activities. She has also begun dating and is making plans for college and a career. However, Jennifer and her parents have been warned by doctors that backsliding is common to her disorder. They need to watch for any changes in Jennifer's behavior or physical appearance. She continues to see a counselor on a regular but not too frequent schedule.

Jennifer's story is an illustration of a serious but not life-threatening case of anorexia nervosa. It has what can be called a happy ending, considering what might have happened to her.

Dying to Be Thin

Alicia is fifteen years old and weighs sixty pounds. She refuses to eat, because, as she says, "Once I start I will just keep gaining weight and gaining weight and it won't stop."[1] She has suffered a heart attack, weakened kidneys, and is blind in one eye. She has been hospitalized about fifty times, during which she was force-fed until her weight returned to a minimum that would allow her to return home. Each time she relapsed and started starving herself again. Her parents are crushed. They are torn between continuing to let Alicia lie in a hospital with tubes in her arm and taking her home to watch her starve to death. Her older sister is resentful of the attention Alicia receives, and her younger brother has told her he wished she would just go away. "Our

*U*nlike some girls, Emmy Pasternak is winning her battle with anorexia nervosa. Emmy's story was made public in an Associated Press interview in which she said her eating disorder was overshadowed by worries about insurance and money for her treatment.

whole life," says her father, "is centered around Alicia and whether she'll keep down what she eats."[2]

Nine years ago Alicia was an outgoing, athletic, happy child. She still has a bulletin board covered with athletic ribbons that she won in grade school. "She was into everything," her sister says. Her mother adds, "She had the highest self-esteem."[3] And then, at summer camp, something happened to change all that. A campmate taunted Alicia about her weight. "She'd say, 'You're too big and you need to lose weight,' and made me drink things and then purge," Alicia remembered.[4] She started cutting back on certain foods—cheese, for example, because it had too much fat, and then candy. Then she stopped eating altogether. About this time her brother was born. Alicia admits that she felt he was getting too much attention. She says she had bad feelings about herself and that she could get rid of them by denying herself food or throwing up what she did eat. Her parents quickly realized they had a problem, and they sought professional help. Her mother feels that Alicia has a fear not only of becoming fat but of growing up.

Alicia knows what is happening to her. Because she has been undergoing treatment for so long, she is familiar with the language of treatment and with therapy. She talks frankly about wanting to get her life back but has become resigned to waiting to die. Alicia comes from a caring, middle-class family that is willing and able to make tremendous efforts to save her.

Recently, Alicia agreed to travel from her home in Florida to New York to be put under the care of a doctor who specializes in treating eating disorders.

Warning Signs of Anorexia Nervosa

✓Refusal to maintain body weight at or above normal minimum weight for age and height

✓Intense fear of gaining weight, or becoming fat, even though underweight

✓Distorted perception of the shape or size of one's body

✓Absence of or disruption of menstruation

✓Binge-eating or purging behavior (self-induced vomiting or misuse of laxatives, diuretics or enemas)

✓Reduction in total food intake

✓Very restricted diet, sometimes limited to only a few foods

✓Increased or excessive exercise

✓Obsessive thoughts about food

Source: Diagnostic and Statistical Manual of Mental Disorders, Fourth Edition (DSM-IV), (Washington, D.C.: American Psychiatric Association, 1994), pp. 539-545.

She welcomed the treatment because "they didn't strap you down and put tubes in your arms."[5] After a few days of the most careful and friendly treatment, she again refused to eat. Her condition got worse, and when she showed signs of kidney failure, the doctor was forced to put her in intensive care and force-feed her. This approach was something that he did only as a last resort and was an indication that the treatment was not working.

Alicia objected violently to the force-feeding and threatened to tear the tubes out of her arm if they were put there. For her, the tubes meant only one thing—putting on weight. When the danger of kidney failure was past, she was taken out of intensive care and returned to her room. There she appeared to recover and began eating again. But it was all a sham, because she purged, or intentionally threw up, everything she ate. She insisted on being sent home, where she felt she could deal with her problem on her own while among family and in familiar surroundings. She was either lying to herself or lying to her family as an excuse to quit the program and go home.

Alicia failed to improve, and her family once again decided, and she agreed, to try another program. This time she was sent to a ranch in Arizona that enforces a program of strict feeding and constant observation. So far, Alicia has regained twenty-five pounds, but it remains to be seen whether this will continue. Whatever the outcome, it is plain that Alicia is in strict control of her life, her family, and her future. She will have to decide whether she wants to live or die.[6] Strangely, she is also out of control because anorexia is what really has a hold over her life, her family, and her future.

*M*any young women who study ballet or gymnastics, which favor a slender body type, find that the pressure to be thin can lead to anorexia.

Like Jennifer, Alicia is suffering from anorexia nervosa. Although Alicia's is an extreme case, it resembles others that have not reached such a serious stage. Anorexics, like Alicia, are mostly white and come from middle-class to upper-class families. Recent research, however, has revealed that the disorder exists among girls and women of other races and among working-class women. This research has gone unreported because the illness was never really understood properly.[7] The patient simply refuses to eat. To just simply about anyone but the person who has this condition, this refusal is hard to believe. Why would anyone not want to eat? Eating is a basic human activity. For some people, it is one of life's main pleasures.

Thin Unto Dying

Eating was a threatening and fearful activity for Samantha Kendall. She was well known in her hometown of Birmingham, England. At one time this thirty-year-old woman had been a nightclub singer, but it wasn't her voice or her good looks that made her so familiar. She was well known because she was starving herself to death.

Samantha was anorexic and believed that eating would make her fat. Anorexics feel that they have no control over their eating habits, and it leads them to avoid food at any cost. At the same time, they have an interest in food and weight that blocks out almost everything else they do and think. This is called a preoccupation, or in the most serious cases, an obsession. Doctors, scientists, and researchers who have studied anorexia nervosa and other eating disorders believe that the victim's preoccupation with food and weight is often a shield to cover up deeper psychological problems. It does not help people like Samantha to point this out to them. They simply cannot stop hating food and their fear of getting fat.

Samantha's twin sister, Michaela, died of anorexia nervosa in April 1994. Samantha seemed to be following in her sister's footsteps. However, a television and newspaper campaign raised enough money to send her to a clinic in Victoria, British Columbia, in Canada. This clinic, the Montreux Counseling Center, had reported amazing results in treating eating disorders through round-the-clock counseling and emotional support. Although the center's claims of success have been questioned by others, its treatment seemed to work for Samantha. She had weighed sixty-three pounds when she entered the clinic in May 1994. Eighteen months later, she returned to England fifty pounds heavier and supposedly cured.

The publicity surrounding her successful recovery made her well known, but she said she felt like "a freak." She believed she would never get rid of the "anorexic" label and that "I'll probably die of anorexia."[8] Soon after returning home, she began starving herself again. In October 1997, she died of liver failure brought on by anorexia nervosa. Again, she made front-page news around the world, focusing attention on this eating disorder. The director of the Montreux clinic, Peggy Claude-Pierre, who claimed to have found the cause and the only sure cure for the disorder, said she was "numbed" by news of Samantha's death.[9] Once again, this baffling illness had defeated the latest and most hopeful method of treatment.

For the families and friends of the more than 5 million Americans who suffer from eating disorders,[10] it was just another story in the long history of one of the cruelest, most heartbreaking, and least understood illnesses. Unlike AIDS, it is not caused by a virus or germ that can be passed from one person to another. Like many other eating disorders, it starts in the mind, and unless it is checked and controlled, it can lead to serious physical and mental damage. Or even, as in the case of Samantha, to death.

Chapter 2

Not Just a Celebrity Sickness

The general public first became aware of anorexia nervosa and other eating disorders in 1983 when the popular singer Karen Carpenter died of heart failure resulting from self-starvation. The year before that, Cherry Boone O'Neill, the daughter of singer and actor Pat Boone, had published a book called *Starving for Attention*. In it she described her long and terrible struggle with eating disorders that had ended with her weighing only eighty pounds and near death in a hospital. The title of her book tells it all. "I was a celebrity's daughter," she wrote. "I thought I had to be perfect."[1] And a large part of perfection, in her mind, was being thin. Cherry O'Neill eventually recovered and went on to lead a normal life and to spread the word about eating disorders. Her book became a best-seller, and she was interviewed on radio and appeared on television talk shows. Her message was heard by hundreds of young girls who recognized O'Neill's disorder as something that was wrong with them also. Some of them had never even heard that anorexia nervosa existed. They thought it was something that only they were experiencing.

It was the death of Karen Carpenter, however, that really caught the world's attention. Why would a young woman who appeared to have everything— youth, good looks, talent, and fame—destroy herself in such a slow and painful way? She did not want to kill herself, but she did have deep problems. She was competitive with her brother and performing partner, Richard. Her brother dominated her career, telling her what to sing and how to sing it. She also had a troubled relationship with her mother, who favored Richard and thought that he was the better musician and singer. She felt that she had no control over the two things that mattered most to her—her voice and her mother's love.[2] Such low self-esteem is one of the main causes of anorexia, and sometimes a single event can trigger it. In Karen's case it was an article in a magazine that referred to her as "chubby."[3] This comment led her to start dieting, that, in turn, began her obsession with food and weight and her long struggle with anorexia. Her heart, though, simply could not stand the strain of performing plus all of life's normal stress and anxiety without eating properly.

With the publicity surrounding the death of Karen Carpenter, other

*A*lthough Karen Carpenter had talent and fame, her low
self-esteem led to a long and tragic battle with anorexia.

celebrities revealed that they, too, had suffered from eating disorders. Actresses Jane Fonda and Susan Dey, champion gymnast Cathy Rigby, and ballet dancer Gelsey Kirkland all told their stories in magazine interviews and on radio and TV appearances. Diana, princess of Wales, also admitted that her eating disorder had complicated her marriage. Many people thought that celebrities' anorexia nervosa and other eating disorders must have been a result of their fame.

What the public did not realize is that eating disorders are not something that only the rich and famous suffer from. There has been a steady and alarming increase in cases of anorexia and other

*C*elebrities such as Jane Fonda have shared their stories of starving themselves to be thin. Fonda now promotes a realistic exercise program and healthful eating habits.

It Can Happen to Anyone

On November 29, 1997, the Swedish royal family announced that Victoria Ingrid Alice Désirée, crown princess of Sweden, was suffering from an eating disorder. "She is receiving therapeutic help," the brief announcement stated. This confirmed rumors that had circulated in the press after Victoria appeared at a ball in a gown that revealed that she was just not thin, but skeletal. The pretty, popular, twenty-year-old heir to the Swedish throne is determined to fulfill her royal obligations. Her sense of duty may pull her through. A nurse and therapist at the Huddinge Hospital Eating Disorders Center in Stockholm, Sweden, says only that Victoria "has great work ahead of her. She must get on with it by first getting well."

Source: "A Slip of a Girl," *People Weekly*, January 12, 1998, pp. 135-137.

eating disorders in this and every other industrialized nation. They have occurred at all levels of society but particularly among the middle class. It is estimated that one to 2 percent of all American women suffer from some form of eating disorder. Some experts who treat people with these disorders place the estimate much higher. The National Institute of Mental Health (NIMH) claims that eating disorders affect more than 5 million Americans each year, and some doctors place the figure at 10 million.[4] NIMH also estimates that one thousand women die each year of anorexia nervosa.

With the publicity given Karen Carpenter and other celebrities, support groups, associations, and organizations have emerged to promote recognition of and treatments for the disorder. Anorexia and other eating disorders are conditions and not diseases that can be clinically treated, the way a doctor would treat a case of measles or mumps. This is the main concern for doctors and clinicians, not to mention patients, parents, and friends. The need for information and knowledge of the causes, therefore, is vital.

Chapter 3

Anorexia Nervosa

Anorexia nervosa, commonly called anorexia, has been around for a long time. However, it was not considered a psychological disorder until about 1974.[1] During the Middle Ages (about A.D. 500 to 1500) it was called *anorexia mirabilis*, or "miraculously inspired," to describe the serious fasting of women who wished to achieve spiritual perfection. Saint Catherine of Siena (1347–1380) ate nothing but a few herbs a day. Fasting became connected with sainthood, and some female saints actually died of starvation.[2] In 1873 an English physician, Sir William Gull, described this "peculiar form of disease" to an audience of interested middle-class women in London, England. That same year Dr. Charles Lasègue described the same "disease" in a medical journal in France.[3] But it was only in the second half of the twentieth century that anorexia gained the attention that it deserves. This has been due mostly to the publicity that newspapers, magazines, and television have given to anorexics, as in the case of Samantha Kendall.

According to the National Association of Anorexia Nervosa and Associated Disorders (ANAD), 7 million girls and women in the United States currently suffer from serious eating disorders. Thirty percent, or more than two hundred thousand, will continue to have difficulties even after diagnosis and treatment. Five to six percent will eventually die from the illness, most from either suicide or heart failure.[4] These figures are much higher than those given by the National Institute of Mental Health, but there are some doctors who feel that the figures are even higher.

Although anorexia is usually thought of as a disorder found among girls and young women, recent studies have shown that boys and men can also suffer from it. The Johns Hopkins Hospital Eating and Weight Disorders Clinic has found that 10 percent of the cases reported to them have been males. This figure is believed to be the same for the nation as a whole.[5] (Note: Because anorexia is still mainly a female disorder, "her" or "she" is used in the text when referring to an anorexic person.)

Although anorexia and other eating disorders have been studied for years, doctors, clinic workers, and researchers cannot agree on what causes them. Anorexia probably begins with a person's feeling about her weight. She might feel that she would look better if she lost a few pounds. Or she may wish to look like some person she admires who weighs less than she does. Over time her opinion of herself may change, and she may think that she can improve herself by losing weight. The obvious way to reduce weight is to eat less or next to nothing at all. At first, this works and the person begins to lose weight.

Eventually, the body adjusts to the reduction in

the amount of food and begins to use less energy to operate. Usually at this point, a person will return to a normal or reduced pattern of eating. But some will be encouraged by the weight loss and decide to continue dieting or even to fast. Their behavior becomes obsessive, and they can think of little else except food and weight loss. They are well on their way to becoming anorexic.

Most experts agree that the continuing desire to lose weight among anorexics results from a mixture of biological, psychological, and environmental causes. A young girl may be teased by her family or friends about her weight, or she may enter into competition with a friend or friends to lose weight. Problems within the family may also bring about stress that may cause the onset of anorexia. Such family disorders as alcohol abuse, arguments over money, or divorce or separation of parents can cause a person to believe that she has no control over her life. Desire to be independent and yet remain within the safe boundaries of her family may also bring about confusion and uncertainty. Or it may be an unlooked-for event or situation, such as a breakup with a boyfriend, a sexual experience, a major school examination, or physical test. Practically anything that is out of the ordinary or beyond the person's ability to handle can cause stress and uncertainty.

Many researchers put part if not all the blame for young girls' preoccupation with their bodies on modern society's ideal of thinness in women. Movie stars, models, dancers, singers, and athletes are held up as role models—and almost all of them are thin. The idea of being "pleasantly plump" has been rejected by most of the entertainment and news media. The "jolly fat person" is known for humor rather than desirability. The message is clear: If a person wants to be popular, successful, famous, or even liked or loved, she must be thin. For many young girls, even being slender is not enough. They want to be thinner, and the only way to do that is to stop eating. Some girls admit to realizing how "revoltingly thin" they look in the mirror but still feel fat.[6]

A distorted, or unreal, body image is another symptom often observed in the anorexic. She sees herself as larger, wider, or fatter than she actually is. No amount of convincing her that she is seeing herself incorrectly does any good. She is sure that her thighs or her hips or her stomach is unnaturally large. She focuses on parts of her body rather than the whole.

Anorexia is difficult to diagnose in the early stages because most anorexics are secretive about their condition. Some go to great lengths to disguise the fact that they are not eating, such as wrapping food in a napkin or keeping it in their mouth and waiting for an opportunity to spit it out. As the disorder progresses, they may eat their food and then get rid of it later by vomiting. Others may disguise their weight loss as the result of dieting or exercise. Once the anorexia becomes advanced, however, it is easy to spot. First is the obvious weight loss. Doctors and researchers have devised tables and charts of desirable weight, according to body build. If a patient's weight falls noticably short of these standards, then anorexia is suspected.

If the girl has started to menstruate, this may cease as she becomes extremely thin—or even before. This signal should be enough to warn her that something is wrong with her body. However, it is usually ignored. As the condition advances, serious changes and damages to the body can take place.

Extreme thinness means that the body no longer has a protective coat of fat to insulate it. As a result, the anorexic feels cold most of the time. Her metabolism also slows, lowering her body temperature. A thin coating of hair may begin to cover her body, which is nature's way of combating the lowered body heat. Dehydration may occur, causing the skin to dry and crack or become discolored. In addition, muscle cramps, hair loss, and a dull or pale complexion may result.

The anorexic also experiences fatigue and a lack of energy. Muscles may waste away, making any

Physical Changes Due to Anorexia Nervosa

✓Emaciated appearance

✓Unexplained, sudden, weight loss

✓Underweight for age and height

✓Depression, social withdrawal, irritability, insomnia

✓Dehydration

✓Constipation, abdominal pain

✓Dryness of skin

Source: Diagnostic and Statistical Manual of Mental Disorders, Fourth Edition (DSM-IV), (Washington, D.C.: American Psychiatric Association, 1994), pp. 539-545.

physical activity extremely tiring and difficult. Not only has menstruation stopped, but so has all sexual activity or desire. Older girls and women may lose the ability to bear children. A shrinkage of internal organs may accompany the shrinkage of body mass and can be permanent. Even if the anorexic recovers, the damage done may not be repaired.

Anorexics may also experience dizziness, light-headedness, constipation, and blackouts. Lowered body resistance makes them extremely open to infection and disease. Death can result if the disease is serious enough. Even if the anorexic remains free from disease, however, the threat of death is ever present. Kidney and heart failure caused by lack of vitamins and minerals can lead to death unless the condition is reversed completely or medical steps such as force-feeding are taken.

Psychological symptoms may include behavior in which anorexics overreact to anything that is said or done to them. They examine and reexamine whatever they have done—whether in words, thoughts, or actions—and usually find that they have failed to do the right thing. They blame themselves for everything negative that has happened to them and refuse to let these feelings go. These feelings can lead to or be accompanied by depression, which is a feeling of dejection or sadness that seems an extreme reaction to whatever caused it.[7] All of this marks a downward path that is heartbreaking to parents and friends, who feel helpless.

Treatment of Anorexia Nervosa

Early recognition and treatment of anorexia is extremely important but difficult because the anorexic often refuses to admit that anything is wrong. Treatment usually consists of medical care through hospitalization or close observance and psychological care through counseling or therapy. Both forms of treatment may be used at the same time. The first objective is to increase the patient's weight and to restore her natural body functions that may have been disrupted by the condition. An anorexic may not be able to think clearly because of the effects of starvation. She first must be nourished enough to be able to make changes.

Hospitalization or close observance by nurses or clinic workers often offers the best hope for the patient's weight gain. Patients are usually given responsibility for resuming normal eating habits. This is difficult because at first most anorexics are not willing to take part in the treatment process. Sometimes they may eat normal meals in order to please their doctors or nurses, and then when they are alone, they purge themselves by vomiting. Therefore, they may require constant watching. If the patient continues to lose weight, force-feeding may be necessary as a last resort to save the anorexic's life.

Meanwhile, doctors, nurses, nutritionists, and counselors try to educate the patient about nutrition and normal eating habits. Their aim is to convince her that she *has* control over her eating behavior. They explain the devastating effects of anorexia on her physical and nervous systems. Then the counselor or someone on the medical team can begin to confront and deal with any family or social problems the patient may have that might have led to her fear of gaining weight. The counselor tries to help her improve her opinion of herself and her body image so that it no longer depends on body weight.

*M*any young women try to attain what society has convinced them is the "ideal" body type—the willowy thinness of a runway model.

Generally, medications are avoided because they may have side effects that could interfere with therapy. However, if the patient suffers depression that persists after initial treatments, an antidepressant such as Prozac may be given to her.

Treatment of anorexia can take a long time. There are so many different things to take into account with each patient that it is impossible to predict either the outcome or the time it will take for that person to be out of danger. Researchers estimate that between 50 and 75 percent of patients suffering from anorexia nervosa will recover completely or become reasonably well enough to lead a normal life. The remaining percentage will continue to have eating disorder problems and will probably have to undergo further therapy. Support groups help in leading the patient away from thinking constantly of food and weight. These groups can also help the patient cope with any personal or social problems that may arise and lead to backsliding.

Treatment of anorexia has become more successful as greater public awareness has lead to earlier detection and diagnosis. More doctors and clinic workers are being trained to deal with eating disorders, and the prospects are good for lowering the death rate. The prevention of eating disorders, however, is another matter. Because there is no definite method of prevention, whether or not a person becomes a victim of the disorder depends on her own awareness of the problem and her willingness to seek help or counseling.

Naomi—In Control?

Naomi was an overachiever. She was an attractive child and was never given any reason to think that

The late Princess Diana, who had once suffered from bulimia, became involved in charity work for organizations like the European Anorexia Trust.

she was of less worth than anyone else. If anything, she was a bit spoiled, with her family and friends constantly praising her. In the third or fourth grade she discovered that she was a natural athlete and was soon playing most team sports, in which she was better than average. At summer camp she learned to swim and became one of the camp's best competitive swimmers. In school she was ranked near the top of her class. She was popular and began dating as soon as she entered high school.

Throughout her elementary and high school years, Naomi had a best friend with whom she spent most of her time. Other friends came and went, but her best friend remained as close to her as at the beginning of their friendship. During their junior year in high school, Naomi's friend began to put on weight. The friend was not too upset by her sudden body change, but Naomi became concerned. She imagined that other people were making fun of them because they had become so different from each other. Even though she remained loyal to her friend, Naomi became determined that what had happened to her friend would not happen to her. She began to cut back on the foods that she and her friend used to enjoy. No more candy or ice cream. No more burgers and fries. Naomi had always been a good runner, so she joined the track team and began to spend most of her free time running around the school track.

By the time she was ready for college, Naomi was slightly underweight. The doctor who examined her for her college physical exam brought this to the attention of her parents. Her parents urged her to eat more but thought that once she got to college she would probably put on weight, as most other girls did when they were served the typically starchy foods of college cafeterias. Naomi and her friend went to different colleges. When they returned home on their first vacation break, the physical differences between them had become even more extreme. Naomi had lost quite a bit of weight, and her friend had gained some more. Naomi was crushed and seemed ashamed, not of her friend but of herself. Her mother noticed that she was not eating, and she had a long talk with her. Naomi assured her that there was nothing wrong and that she was just stressed out at her new school.

Naomi's freshman year at college was unsatisfactory. She spent all her time running and working out at the college gym. Her grades were average but far from what her family had expected of her. At the end of her freshman year, she told her parents that she was dropping out for a while. She would get a job and then return to school after a year or so. Naomi's mother began to suspect that her daughter was throwing up her food. Naomi again assured her mother that nothing was wrong, she was just nervous and anxious about being away from home and that she would soon be back to normal.

Naomi did regain some weight, but she was still thinner than she had been in high school. She did not return to college but took a job in nearby New York City. True to form, she excelled in her job and received raises that made her financially independent of her parents. She moved out of her parents' house and rented an apartment in the city. She was now completely on her own and alone, without anyone questioning her eating behavior. Before long, she became engaged and moved in with her fiancé. She began cooking elaborate meals for him, revealing a knowledge of food and cooking that no one had suspected. She did not eat much herself, however. In fact, she did not eat anything. She became thinner and thinner. After many arguments with her fiancé over her eating behavior, she broke off their engagement. She also decided to return to college, and she quit her job and returned to live with her parents.

Naomi began to change. Whether it was the result of counseling, reading and learning about eating disorders, or personal experience, she resumed eating in small amounts. Whatever caused the change may have been as simple as the desire not to be fat that triggered her anorexia. Or it could have been an unpleasant event such as the breakup with her fiancé. She herself doesn't know and can't explain the reasons for the change in her behavior.

Naomi is about to graduate from college. She is in the top 10 percent of her class and should have little trouble in obtaining employment in whatever field she chooses. She has regained some weight but still looks thin and undernourished. She is not in danger of losing her life, but some damage has been done to her body's system. She is late in returning to her normal menstrual cycle. She also has dental problems due to her frequent vomiting during her illness. Stomach acid can eat away tooth enamel.

Whether Naomi goes on to make something of herself and her life remains up to her. She has been offered all the medical and counseling help that is available, but she has refused to undergo therapy. She has been supplied with all the books, videos, and printed programs available on the subject, and she is fully aware of what she has done and may do to herself. It is entirely up to her.

Anorexia in Males

Anorexia nervosa is a disorder occurring primarily in adolescent girls, but older women and men also suffer from this illness. Thinness has never been a male ideal in the same way that it is for young women. Many young men want to increase their weight rather than decrease it. To be "skinny" is not what the average teenage boy wants to be. He usually wants to be rugged or muscular. Magazines, newspaper articles, and television shows that are marketed toward young men do not emphasize diet and clothing to make them appear attractive. The slightly overweight "pudgy" male is not viewed as negatively as an overweight female would be.

Male anorexics are more likely to be very overweight or obese, and their self-starving may be an extreme method of attaining a desirable body image. In this respect they are no different from adolescent girls. They hate fat and fear food. Only about 5 percent of anorexics are men, and many are people who have a professional interest in keeping their weight low. Models, dancers, jockeys, wrestlers, swimmers, and men in the entertainment world may adopt the same patterns and strategies as female anorexics.[8] The motivation of these men, however, seems practical rather than mental or emotional. This is not to say that some male adolescents do not go through the same emotional, social, or family situations that may trigger an eating disorder as young women do.[9] However, the main concern of the medical and psychiatric institutions as well as the public at large is for the adolescent girl.

Chapter 4

Bulimia Nervosa

Bulimia nervosa is an eating disorder in which a person indulges in binge eating and purging. She eats as much as she can in a short time, and then feels so guilty that she tries to eliminate what she has eaten by vomiting, taking laxatives, exercising more than normal, or fasting. It is similar to anorexia nervosa in the way the subject uses self-destructive eating patterns to deal with personal, family, or social problems. It occurs most often among women in their late teens or early twenties. Bulimia differs from anorexia because it is not as easily identified in its advanced stages. A bulimic person may appear perfectly normal, or even a little overweight.[1]

The word *bulimia* comes from the Greek words for ox or cow and hunger. It means eating like an ox, or overeating, something that people have been doing for centuries. Overeating followed by purging was common in ancient Rome, where separate rooms called vomitoriums were built next to banquet halls. Diners could go there to purge themselves so that they could return to the dining hall to eat more food. It was considered a compliment to their host to eat as much as possible. Gluttony, or excessive overeating, was common enough in the Middle Ages for the Catholic Church to consider it a major sin. It was not until 1979 that an English doctor named Gerald Russell noted an "ominous variation" in some of his patients suffering from anorexia nervosa.[2] They would frequently go on eating binges, only to purge themselves afterward by making themselves vomit. Although some anorexia patients occasionally binge eat and then purge themselves, they do not do so regularly. Dr. Russell considered this regular binge eating and purging a separate disorder, which he named bulimia. It was later given the full name bulimia nervosa.[3]

Once the disorder was identified, it was learned that bulimia nervosa is four to six times as common as anorexia nervosa.[4] A separate list of warning signs for diagnosing bulimia was adopted by the American College of Psychiatrists in the early 1990s. First is evidence of the bulimic's consumption of a great deal of food over a short time (usually less than two hours). She lacks control of her eating over that period—she can't help herself. She regularly resorts to extreme measures to control her weight: self-induced vomiting, overuse of laxatives, strict dieting, fasting, and vigorous exercise. All this is related to a constant concern about her body weight and shape, even though she may appear perfectly normal.

Physical symptoms of bulimia are likely to be centered in the digestive system. Stomach pain, constipation, and indigestion may occur separately or all at once. More alarming are the vomiting of blood, swollen glands in neck and face, broken blood vessels, dry and flaky skin, and loss of tooth enamel (due to contact with stomach acids resulting from vomiting), which can lead to decay. Along with all of these are psychological factors such as mood swings, depression, and overall weakness or exhaustion. None of these are pleasant, but they can go undetected if the bulimic is careful or clever enough to hide them from others.

The medical consequences of bulimia can be

Warning Signs of Bulimia Nervosa

✓Recurrent episodes of binge-eating behavior (eating excessively in a short period of time)

✓Sense of lack of control over eating (feeling that one cannot stop eating or control what or how much one is eating)

✓Self-induced vomiting, misuse of laxatives, diuretics, enemas or other medications

✓Self-image is negatively influenced by body shape and weight

✓Fasting for a day or more

✓Attempt to conceal symptoms

✓Exercising excessively

Source: Diagnostic and Statistical Manual of Mental Disorders, Fourth Edition (DSM-IV), (Washington, D.C.: American Psychiatric Association, 1994), pp. 545-550.

*P*eople who suffer from bulimia nervosa go on eating binges during which they consume unusually large amounts of food in a short time.

dehydration (loss of body fluids) and damage to bowels, liver, and kidneys. The disrupting of the body's system created by alternate binge eating and purging can often lead to an irregular heartbeat and in extreme cases to cardiac arrest.[5] If bulimia exists in combination with anorexia nervosa, however, it can complicate that condition and increase the possibility of collapse and death.

Treatment of Bulimia Nervosa

The treatment of bulimia depends on the individual patient. There is such a wide variation in the eating behaviors of bulimics and the physical changes that can take place over a long period, that no set procedure is adequate. Several self-help manuals are available for the use of anyone willing to follow these programs.

If the patient requires or seeks professional help, the clinic worker will try to get her weight within a normal range for her body build and type. A therapist, dietitian, counselor, or other interested person attempts to reduce the patient's constant thinking about food. They try to teach her ways to develop a new attitude toward eating as it relates to body weight and shape. The patient will be encouraged not to weigh herself every day, but only once a week, for example. Other compulsive or habitual behaviors such as studying recipes, trying new diets, cooking new foods, and counting calories will be discouraged. The therapist may have her keep a diary in which she records her moods and the food she eats so she will recognize how they are related. The idea is to separate the idea of food from mood. All this is done to set up a normal pattern in the patient's relationship with food.

A more difficult and essential task is to get the patient to realize that food is not a solution to her problems. If she can understand what her problems are, then perhaps she can find a way to cope with them other than binge eating. Some doctors and researchers believe that low self-esteem is one of the primary causes of eating disorders. Others believe that the victims of these disorders are too young to have yet developed a strong sense of self. However, gaining control of one's own behavior cannot help but raise a person's self-confidence. This is what the concerned people involved are trying to do for the bulimic patient.

Jodi—Feeling Good About Herself

Jodi Miller was an attractive twenty-eight-year-old blond who was five feet nine inches tall and weighed 165 pounds. From all appearances, she was popular and outgoing and had no reasons to feel unhappy. But she thought she was fat, impossibly fat. Every time she looked in the mirror she was displeased with what she saw. She started dieting and

Physical and Psychological Changes Due to Bulimia Nervosa

✓Generally within the normal weight range, but may be slightly underweight or overweight

✓Low self-esteem

✓Depression

✓Dental enamel erosion

✓Scars or calluses on hand from contact with the teeth when inducing vomiting

✓Substance abuse problems, especially of stimulants

Source: Diagnostic and Statistical Manual of Mental Disorders, Fourth Edition (DSM-IV), (Washington, D.C.: American Psychiatric Association, 1994), pp. 545-550.

exercising to the point of exhaustion. At one point, she went on a complete fast. But in her mind it was not having any effect. No matter what size dress, blouse, or sweater she wore, it was too large. She wanted to wear a size ten dress, but at one point she was a size eighteen. No one criticized her or made remarks about her weight. Her boyfriend thought she was beautiful, but she was convinced that she was ugly and fat. She became so depressed and desperate to be thin that she decided that she could no longer consume food.

During a frightening two-year period, Jodi became bulimic. She tried to purge herself of everything she ate by vomiting. She knew that it was disgusting, but she forced herself to throw up four to five times a day. She became thinner, but not so much that it was particularly noticeable. She appeared to be on a downhill spiral. What saved her was the support she received from her boyfriend, Steve, who was later to become her husband. From the beginning of her depression, Steve had tried to convince her that she was everything he desired in a woman. To him, she was perfect just the way she was. With his help she finally realized that she could not get any thinner no matter how hard she tried. Steve persuaded her to send pictures of herself to a modeling agency called Plus Models. This is a company that specializes in placing models with "full figures" for use by the fashion industry. She eventually traveled to New York City for a photo session from which she put together a portfolio. She has since signed a contract with Plus Models and is looking forward to a full-time career in modeling.

One of the encouraging things about Jodi's story is that she has become part of a movement in fashion and advertising circles that is working to convince the public that the average size of a woman is not a size ten but a size twelve or larger. As one editor of a fashion magazine has said, they are fighting against the "size bigotry" that completely ignores the healthy woman who doesn't happen to match the standard image of the superthin models who appear in almost all fashion advertising.[6] This new attitude toward body image may not cure many bulimics, but it at least can start them on the way to constructing a better opinion of themselves. Jodi's story was also told on national television, another encouraging sign that people are finally becoming aware of the alarming danger of eating disorders.[7]

Chapter 5

Other Eating Disorders

Although anorexia nervosa and bulimia nervosa are the most well-known eating disorders, there are other equally serious disorders that affect the physical and emotional health of those who suffer from them.

Binge-Eating Disorder

Binge-eating disorder is much like bulimia but is considered a separate disorder by doctors. Binge eaters, like bulimics, consume great amounts of food in a short period, but unlike bulimics they do not purge. Binge eaters have been known to consume the entire contents of a refrigerator, regardless of whether or not they liked the foods. After a binge, they may suffer aftereffects like those experienced by heavy drinkers or alcoholics. Binges are often followed by extreme feelings of shame or guilt. Binge eaters may be unable to function normally after an eating episode, causing them to miss work or school.

Although very little is known about binge eating,

Warning Signs of a Binge-Eating Disorder

✓ Eating an abnormally large amount of food within a small period of time (usually less than two hours)

✓ Feeling as if one has no control during a binge-eating episode

✓ Eating too quickly

✓ Eating until uncomfortably full

✓ Eating a lot when not physically hungry

✓ Eating alone, due to embarrassment over one's binge eating

✓ Feeling disgusted, depressed, or guilty during and after binge-eating episodes

✓ Concerns about effect of binge-eating episodes on weight and body shape

✓ Binge eating is sustained for at least two days a week for six months

✓ One usually does not purge, fast, or exercise excessively to compensate for binge eating

Source: Diagnostic and Statistical Manual of Mental Disorders, Fourth Edition (DSM-IV), (Washington, D.C.: American Psychiatric Association, 1994), pp. 729-731.

it is considered a way some people cope with personal problems. It is estimated that 2 percent of Americans are affected. They may make up as much as 30 percent of all persons who engage in weight-control programs in hospitals.[1] Binge eaters usually experience weight changes of ten to twenty pounds or more. Binge eating may occur, on the average, at least two days a week, and each binge may last two hours.[2]

Frequent changes in body weight can interfere with the body's metabolism, the process by which the body converts food into energy. If more food is consumed than is needed by the body, it is stored as fat. If less food is consumed, as during a diet, the body burns the excess fat. Binging and dieting can disrupt this process, making it more difficult for the body to maintain normal body functions such as digestion, blood circulation, breathing, and all the others that make for a healthy body.

Obesity and Compulsive Overeating

Obesity is not an eating disorder but a body condition. However, a fear of becoming obese is one of the main causes of eating disorders. Most doctors and researchers agree that obesity occurs when a person weighs 20 percent more than the ideal body weight for his or her body frame. A person who fears becoming obese may start dieting or try other means of weight control. This fear can start early in life among overweight children who are teased by other children. They may be made to feel insecure about their appearance and may not want to participate in sports or other activities important to young people. They may become habitual dieters, constantly gaining and losing weight. This can lead to eating disorders such as bulimia or compulsive overeating.

A compulsion is an irresistible desire to do something, regardless of the effect it may have on the person doing it.

Alcoholics, for example, have an overwhelming

*D*r. Louis Tartaglia of Millennium Pharmaceuticals, Inc., holds a container with three lab mice being used in the search for a drug to help treat human obesity.

desire to drink, no matter what effect it may have on them or the people they are close to. Compulsive eaters have the same uncontrollable desire, usually due to some psychological reason.

Many doctors and researchers believe that obesity is due to heredity rather than overeating. For example, if a person's parents are overweight, he or she will probably be overweight, too. Although there is no denying that large parents usually have large children, the children will not always become obese. It is thought, rather, that their bodies are programmed to make more efficient use of the food they eat, so they do not burn as many calories as other people for the same amount of energy they use. Therefore, what is left over is stored as fat. Unfortunately, anxiety over possible obesity may trigger unhealthful eating habits, or even compulsive overeating. So far, no one knows the percentage of overweight people who are fat due to heredity.[3]

Compulsive overeaters may not suffer from the serious effects of anorexia or bulimia, but they often have medical problems. If they become obese, the extra weight will put a strain on the heart, which can cause serious heart conditions. Compulsive eating over a long period can lead to high blood pressure and diabetes. Also, because they may binge on food that they enjoy—candy, junk food, or one particular favorite food—malnutrition may result.

Regardless of the emotional, psychological, social, or genetic causes of obesity, the treatment is weight reduction. This is not easy, as any dieter knows. The process is a slow one, aiming at gradual weight reduction rather than a sudden and dramatic shedding of excess pounds. A person should lose one to two pounds a week at most.

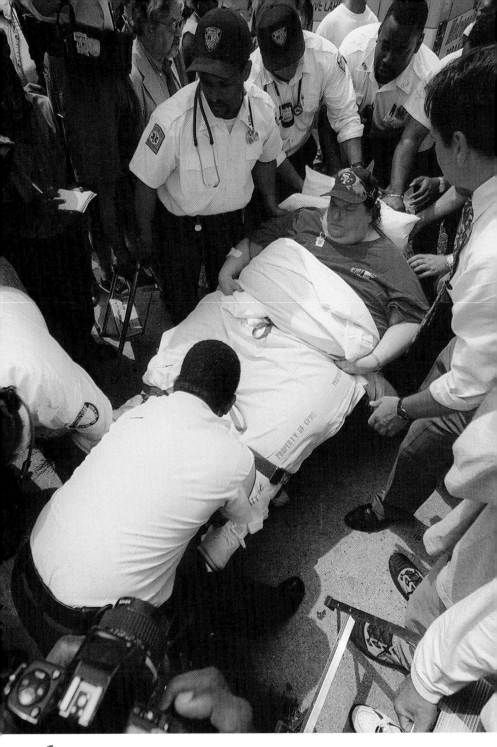

*I*n 1996, Michael Hebranko returns to his home after losing three hundred pounds while hospitalized. Two months before, he had weighed about eight hundred pounds.

Eating Disorders in Women Ages 15 to 30

✓ Anorexia nervosa . . . . 0.5–1.0 percent

✓ Bulimia nervosa . . . . 2 percent

✓ Binge-eating disorder . . . . 15 percent

✓ Obesity . . . . 5 percent

Source: Suzanne Abraham and Derek Llewellyn-Jones, *Eating Disorders— The Facts*, (New York: Oxford University Press, 1997), p. 34.

A good weight-reducing program aims at convincing the subject to eat less and resist the urge to overeat. It should also make it clear to the patient that he or she often underestimates the amount that they eat. Fixed guidelines for food consumption should be set and followed.

A weight-reducing program should start with a menu plan that offers a wide variety of food choices. These foods should be nutritionally well balanced but low in energy-producing fats and simple carbohydrates such as bread and sweets. The diet plan should supply less than the person's energy requirements. Above all, it should be acceptable to the person and be presented in a way that does not make it so different from what other people are eating. It must be continued for at least four weeks so that sudden changes in weight can be averaged out and definite results can be determined.

The second part of a weight-reduction program is exercise. Many obese people are accused of being lazy or lacking in energy. Such accusations, particularly if they are made to youngsters, may cause embarrassment, shame, or low self-esteem. These may, in turn, cause an eating disorder such as bulimia or compulsive eating. Whether or not the accusations are true, a person who does not exercise is not going to burn up the energy that is produced by the food he or she eats. An exercise program should be fairly strenuous and regular. Walking, swimming, and jogging are probably the easiest and most pleasurable and satisfying exercise activities. Because they may be done alone, there is no competitiveness, as in team sports, or comparisons with others who may be more graceful or athletic.

Pica

One of the most unusual eating disorders is called pica, after the Latin word for magpie, a crowlike bird known for eating anything and everything. People suffering from this disorder have a craving to eat things that are considered inedible. These can include dirt, clay, starch, chalk, paper, paint, sand, soap, cigarettes, and just about anything else that can be put in the mouth, chewed, and swallowed. It is an ancient disorder that was described by the Greek father of medicine, Hippocrates.

Eating dirt and clay is known as geophagia and is practiced by pregnant women in the southern United States as well as in Africa. It has also been observed in nonpregnant and nonnursing mothers and in children as well as people suffering from mental handicaps. Some earth and clay eaters believe that they relieve nausea and diarrhea, increase salivation, and remove poisons from the blood. Actually, they can cause an iron deficiency by binding iron in the intestines. They can also cause digestive problems, dental injury, and poisoning. Surgery may be required in some cases to remove indigestible substances from the stomach or intestines.

The causes of the dangerous practice of pica are unknown. The most common explanation for it is that it is due to emotional disturbances and malnutrition, resulting from a lack of iron or zinc in the diet. Another theory is that it is a cultural feature in certain religions, folk medicine, and magic.

Psychologists believe that it is a person's response to stress. Others believe that it is just a bad habit. Whatever its cause, it is a serious, dangerous disorder and doctors and clinicians have no treatment except psychological counseling and constant supervision of the patients' eating behavior.[4]

Chapter 6

Coping

All eating disorders are complicated, and not all can be treated alike. Most experts agree that eating disorders arise from psychological problems caused by cultural forces and social pressures over which victims have no control. However, one cannot change our culture and society in order to deal with one group of people's problems. To reverse our culture's ideal of slimness over fatness would take decades and even centuries, provided that everyone agreed that the change was preferable. Some advances have been made, however, and attitudes may be changing. Omega, a Swiss manufacturer of watches, withdrew its advertising from *Vogue* magazine because it featured ultrathin models showing off the advertisers' products.[1] Omega's spokesperson said it was irresponsible for the magazine to use models of anorexic proportions, which could encourage eating disorders in young women. But possible future change does not help someone who is in the grip of an eating disorder right now.

Most observers agree that eating disorders are psychological problems best dealt with in therapy. There are three main methods of treating eating disorders: (1) cognitive-behavioral therapy, (2) supportive psychotherapy, and (3) behavioral therapy.

The first of these, *cognitive-behavioral therapy*, appears to be the most successful,[2] although it may be used in combination with the other two. To be cognitive means that something is known and is understood. Therefore, it is believed, if you know and understand your behavior, it can be controlled and, if necessary, changed. In treating eating disorders by this method, the therapist, a known and trusted individual, supplies the patient with accurate information about her condition and tries to help her change her behavior.

Cognitive-behavioral therapy is a slow and careful process that can take four to five months or longer. The patient meets with his or her therapist once or twice a week. In that time they discuss the patient's thoughts, beliefs, and feelings about food, eating behavior, and weight control. The therapist explains everything he or she knows about these matters and tries to get the patient to understand the importance of establishing healthful eating habits. Throughout these sessions, the therapist attempts to help the patient follow regular eating habits. Along with the discussion of food and eating, there is also an attempt to help the patient to think more highly of herself and not to put such value on personal appearance. The goal is to raise her self-esteem. Knowledge and understanding are seen as the keys to changing her behavior.

Supportive psychotherapy is used in treating a patient who has an immediate problem due to

The news that Swiss watchmaker Omega pulled its ads from *Vogue* in protest against pictures of extremely thin models made the front page of several British newspapers.

some social or personal crisis that leads her to adopt a destructive eating behavior. The patient may be someone who has recovered or is recovering from an eating disorder and who has taken up her old habits in response to the crisis. The therapist talks to and listens to the patient over a long period. The therapist encourages the patient to talk about her problem and advises her on how to change her behavior. The goal is for the patient to discover that she can cope with the stress and anxiety caused by her personal problems without going back to her old eating habits. This treatment is usually used in combination with cognitive-behavior therapy.

Behavior therapy is based on the reward method of changing a harmful pattern of behavior. An anorexic, for example, is confined to an environment where he or she can be observed, such as a hospital room. She is encouraged to change her eating behavior by her therapist or doctor, who uses the techniques of other therapies that seem to work. If the patient responds by eating more or regularly, for example, she is rewarded by an easing of restrictions or the granting of privileges. This can be a very strict and rigid therapy, but if the patient shows improvement, it becomes less harsh and more relaxed. This treatment is effective with bulimics, who must be watched closely to see that they do not purge after eating.

There are other therapies that involve long periods of time and commitment by both therapist and patient, but these can be very expensive. They treat eating disorders as personality disorders and resemble psychoanalytic treatment programs.

Fortunately, a network of support groups has developed throughout the United States and abroad

Recommended Calorie Intake

	Age	Weight (pounds)	Height (inches)	Calorie Needs Average/Range
Males	11–14	99	62	2700/2000-3900
	15–18	145	69	2800/2100-3900
	19–22	154	70	2900/2500-3300
	23–50	154	70	2700/2300-3100
Females	11–14	101	62	2200/1500-3000
	15–18	120	64	2100/1200-3000
	19–22	120	64	2100/1700-2500
	23–50	120	64	2100/1600-2400

Source: Boston Children's Hospital.

to help people who are recovering or have recovered from eating disorders. Support groups are like group therapy meetings except they are usually not supervised by professionals. The members meet as regularly as they can and exchange information, share experiences, and lend their support to one another. If someone fears that she is in danger of going back to her old eating habits, a fellow member of the group is available to call and talk over the problem. Together they try to find some solution that does not center on food.

Support groups have found an excellent way to reach out to people with eating disorders: the Internet. Several Web sites now exist that provide counseling, encouragement, sympathy, and information to anyone with an actual or suspected eating disorder. Apparently, many secret food bingers and bulimics are not so secretive about their disorder when it comes to chatting on the Internet. This openess is very encouraging because early recognition of an eating disorder is the first step in successful treatment. However, without supervision by a therapist, there is always the chance that a person will not receive the special care that she may need.

Finally, there is the medical treatment of eating disorders. The most commonly used drugs for combating binge eating and bulimia nervosa, and in some cases anorexia nervosa, are antidepressants. Studies have shown that 50 to 90 percent of patients with bulimia binge less when they are treated with antidepressants.[3] Not all patients react the same way to any particular antidepressant, so several may be tried before one is found that is effective. The required dosage may also vary among patients, so it may take some time to find the right amount to use. All this can be expensive and in some cases dangerous because there are side effects to many antidepressants.

Nevertheless, antidepressants may stop bulimics from binging. They may also lessen depression and feelings of hopelessness. Or they may simply help a person feel better about herself or about life in general. One of the most successful drugs in treating eating disorders, and the only one that seems to help anorexics, is Prozac.[4] This drug may lessen the patient's preoccupation with food and body image and thus make it easier to proceed with further treatment such as cognitive-behavioral therapy. Prozac also has mild side effects but does not have a sedative or tranquilizing effect.

The search for a physical cause for eating disorders and for a drug or medication that will prevent or cure them continues. Research into the lack of balance in body chemicals as the cause is now being conducted.

In February 1999, a study published in the *American Medical Association's Archives of General Psychiatry* indicated that bulimia may be triggered by a lack of tryptophan in the brain. Tryptophan is an amino acid, or part of a protein, that is used to make serotonin by the body. Serotonin is a chemical found in the brain that regulates mood and appetite. The study found that women who were deprived of tryptophan were more likely to worry about their body image and whether they have control over their eating habits.[5]

Studies of body changes that can lead to distaste or disgust with food are also being carried out, with the hope that they will lead to a cure by increasing or decreasing the amount of the hormone estrogen in the body. All this is encouraging and a sign that the medical and mental health organizations and institutions are aware that eating disorders are a serious problem. They are beginning to be taken as seriously as any other illness or disease that is life-threatening.

The increase in public awareness and the attention that eating disorders are receiving in the media have given help and encouragement to many people who thought they suffered alone and were somehow to blame for their condition. It has also helped many sufferers understand that they themselves play a large part in the solution to their problems. It is their willingness to participate in the recovery process that is the first step to a cure.

Organizations

American Anorexic Bulimia Association, Inc. (AABA)
165 W. Forty-sixth Street, Suite 1108
New York, NY 10036
(212) 575-6200

Anorexia Nervosa and Related Eating Disorders (ANRED)
P.O. Box 5102
Eugene, OR 97405
(541) 344-1144

Massachusetts Eating Disorders Association, Inc. (MEDA)
1162 Beacon Street
Brookline, MA 02146
(617) 558-1881

National Association of Anorexia Nervosa
& Associated Disorders (ANAD)
P.O. Box 7
Highland Park, IL
(847) 831-3438

National Eating Disorders Organization (NEDO)
6655 S. Yale Avenue
Tulsa, OK 74136
(918) 481-4044

Any of the above can provide information on local support groups and listings of therapists and hospitals.

Web Sites

Anorexia and Bulimia Family Support Group
 <http://users.iafrica.com/r/ro/ronhey/main.htm>

The Something Fishy Website on Eating Disorders
 <http://www.something-fishy.org>
This is one of the most popular and useful support groups.

Chapter 1. A Baffling Illness

1. "Dying to Be Thin," *48 Hours*, CBS-TV, broadcast Thursday, February 26, 1998.

2. Ibid.

3. Ibid.

4. Ibid.

5. Ibid.

6. Ibid.

7. Beatrice Trim Hunter, "Eating Disorders: Perilous Compulsions," *Consumers' Research*, September 1997, p. 11.

8. "Anorexia's Victory," *Maclean's*, November 10, 1997, p. 47.

9. Ibid.

10. American Anorexia Bulimia Association, Inc., *Facts on Eating Disorders*, bulletin, 1997, p. 1.

Chapter 2. Not Just a Celebrity Sickness

1. Cherry Boone O'Neill, *Starving for Attention* (New York: Continuum Publishing Company, 1982), p. 29.

2. Rob Hoerburger, "Karen Carpenter's Second Life," *The New York Times Magazine*, October 6, 1996, p. 54.

3. Jane E. Brody, "A Nationwide Program Aims to Help Young People Who Are Beset by Eating Disorders," *The New York Times*, January 31, 1996, p. 16.

4. "Dying to Be Thin," *48 Hours*, CBS-TV, broadcast Thursday, February 26, 1998.

Chapter 3. Anorexia Nervosa

1. Rachel Epstein, *Eating Habits and Disorders* (New York: Chelsea House Publishers, 1990), p. 35.

2. Dana K. Cassell with E. F. Larocca, *Encyclopedia of Obesity and Eating Disorders* (New York: Facts On File, 1994), p. 11.

3. Epstein, pp. 34–35.

4. Betsy Streisand, "Overcoming Anorexia," *U.S. News & World Report*, September 29, 1997, p. 67.

5. American Anorexia Bulimia Association, Inc., "Males and Eating Disorders: Critical Questions," *Facts on Eating Disorders*, bulletin, 1997, p. 4.

6. Suzanne Abraham and Derek Llewellyn-Jones, *Eating Disorders—The Facts* (New York: Oxford University Press, 1997), p. 90

7. Steven Levenkron, *Obsessive-Compulsive Disorders* (New York: Warner Books, 1991), p. 1.

8. Susan Gilbert, "More Men May Be Seeking Eating-Disorder Help," *The New York Times*, August 28, 1996, p. D2.

9. American Anorexia Bulimia Association, Inc., "Males and Eating Disorders: Critical Questions," pp. 4–5.

Chapter 4. Bulimia Nervosa

1. American Anorexia Bulimia Association, Inc., *Facts on Eating Disorders*, bulletin, 1997, p. 1.

2. Suzanne Abraham and Derek Llewellyn-Jones, *Eating Disorders—The Facts* (New York: Oxford University Press, 1997), p. 26.

3. Ibid., p. 26.

4. Ibid., p. 27.

5. American Anorexia Bulimia Association, Inc., p. 1.

6. "Dying to Be Thin," 48 Hours, CBS-TV, broadcast Thursday, February 26, 1998.

7. Ibid.

Chapter 5. Other Eating Disorders

1. Beatrice Trim Hunter, "Eating Disorders: Perilous Compulsions," *Consumers' Research*, September 1997, p. 12.

2. Suzanne Abraham and Derek Llewellyn-Jones, *Eating Disorders—The Facts* (New York: Oxford University Press, 1997), p. 18.

3. Ibid., pp. 183–185.

4. Hunter, p. 13.

Chapter 6. Coping

1. "Skeletal Models Create Furor over British *Vogue*," *The New York Times*, June 3, 1996, p. C2.

2. Suzanne Abraham and Derek Llewellyn-Jones, *Eating Disorders—The Facts* (New York: Oxford University Press, 1997), p. 73.

3. Diane Mickley, "Eating Disorders & Antidepressants," *Facts on Eating Disorders*, American Anorexia Bulimia Association, Inc., bulletin, 1997, p. 2.

4. Ibid., p. 3.

5. "Study Links Bulimia to Chemical Malfunction in the Brain." *The New York Times*, February 16, 1999, p. F12.

anorexia nervosa—An eating disorder in which a person starves him or herself or eats very little in order to lose weight.

backsliding—When someone who has had an eating disorder in the past begins exhibiting symptoms again.

binge-eating disorder—An eating disorder in which a person consumes large amounts of food in a short amount of time, but does not purge.

body image—How someone sees him or herself physically.

bulimia nervosa—An eating disorder in which a person indulges in binge eating and purging.

compulsive overeating—An eating disorder in which a person has an uncontrollable desire to overeat, usually due to some psychological reason.

counselor—A professional who helps someone deal with the psychological problems that influence an eating disorder, as well as the mental stresses of battling an eating disorder.

dehydration—When the body loses essential fluids.

dietitian—A professional who advises a person on how to eat healthy.

fasting—Not eating for a certain, extended period of time.

force-feeding—Feeding an eating disorder patient through a needle when he or she refuses to eat.

geophagia—The practice of eating earth or clay.

laxative—A drug which is meant to relieve constipation.

metabolism—The combination of the biological processes that take place in the body.

obesity—A condition where a person weighs about 20 percent more than his or her ideal weight.

obsession—When someone can't stop thinking about something.

pica—An eating disorder in which a person eats inedible substances.

purging—Intentionally throwing up.

refeeding—A treatment for anorexics where the patient eats under close supervision.

self-esteem—How one feels about him or herself.

Abraham, Suzanne, and Derek Llewellyn-Jones. *Eating Disorders—The Facts,* 4th ed. New York: Oxford University Press, 1997.

Bode, Janet. *Food Fight*. New York: Simon & Schuster, 1997.

Burby, Liza N. *Bulimia Nervosa: The Secret Cycle of Bingeing & Purging*. New York: Rosen Publishing Group, Inc., 1998.

Cassell, Dana K., with E. F. Larocca, M.D., F.A.P. *Encyclopedia of Obesity and Eating Disorders.* New York: Facts On File, 1994.

Epstein, Rachel. *Eating Habits and Disorders*. New York: Chelsea House Publishers, 1990.

Erlanger, Ellen. *Eating Disorders: A Question and Answer Book About Anorexia Nervosa and Bulimia Nervosa*. Minneapolis, Minn.: Lerner Publications, 1988.

Frissell, Susan, and Paula Harney. *Eating Disorders and Weight Control*. Springfield, N.J.: Enslow Publishers, Inc., 1998.

Maloney, Michael, M.D., and Rachel Kranz. *Straight Talk About Eating Disorders*. New York: Facts On File, 1991.

Nardo, Dan. *Eating Disorders*. San Diego, Calif.: Lucent Books, Inc., 1991.

Sneddon, Pamela Shires. *Body Image: A Reality Check*. Springfield, N.J.: Enslow Publishers, Inc., 1998.

Further Reading